Campaspe by John Lyly

Played beefore the Queenes Majesty on new yeares day at night, by her Majestys Children, and the Children of Paules.

John Lyly was born in Kent in 1553 or 1554, the eldest of eight children.

As can be imagined accurate records dating so far back of his early life are few and far between. It is most probable that Canterbury, Kent was his actual birthplace.

At age sixteen he became a student at Magdalen College, Oxford, and obtained his bachelor's degree in 1573 and his master's two years later.

Lyly became the private secretary of Lord Burghley's son-in-law, Edward de Vere, 17th Earl of Oxford, himself a playwright (and to whom the second part of 'Euphues' is dedicated).

He began his own literary career with 'Euphues', or 'The Anatomy of Wit', which was published in the spring of 1579.

'Euphues and his England' appeared in 1580, and, like the first part of the book, won immediate popularity. For a time Lyly was the most successful and fashionable of English writers, hailed as the author of 'a new English'.

After the publication of 'Euphues' Lyly changed literary direction; from writing novels to writing plays.

His 'Campaspe' and 'Sapho and Phao' were produced at Court in 1582. In total, probably eight Lyly plays were acted before the queen by the Children of the Chapel and by the Children of Paul's between the years 1584 and 1591, and some repeated before a popular audience at the Blackfriars Theatre. Lyly used quick, lively dialogue, classical colour and frequent references to people and events of the day that sustained his popularity with the court which 'Euphues' had won.

Aside from his writing Lyly also sat in parliament as a member for Hindon in Wiltshire in 1580, for Aylesbury in Buckinghamshire in 1593, for Appleby in Westmorland in 1597 and finally for Aylesbury again in 1601.

After 1590 his works steadily declined in influence and he in reputation although he continued to serve in parliament; in 1598 he served on a parliamentary committee about wine abuse.

In the early weeks of November 1606, John Lyly passed away from an unknown disease. He was buried in London at St Bartholomew-the-Less on 20th November 1606.

Index of Contents

DRAMATIS PERSONAE

Alexander, King of Macedon
Page to Alexander
Melippus, Chamberlain to Alexander
Hephestion, his General
Alexander's Warriors:
Clytus, an officer
Parmenio, an officer
Milectus, a soldier
Phrygius, a soldier
Philosophers:
Plato.
Granichus, Servant to Plato
Aristotle
Diogenes
Manes, Servant to Diogenes

Chrysippus
Crates
Cleanthes
Anaxarchus
Apelles, a Painter
Psyllus, Servant to Apelles
Crysus, a beggar
Solinus, a citizen of Athens
Sylvius, a citizen of Athens
Perim, Son to Sylvius
Milo, Son to Sylvius
Trico, Son to Sylvius
Lais, a Courtesan
Campaspe, a Theban Captive
Timoclea, a Theban Captive
Citizens of Athens, other captive women, etc

SCENE: Athens.

THE PROLOGUE AT THE BLACKE FRYERS

They that fear the stinging of wasps make fans of peacocks' tails, whose spots are like eyes. And Lepidus, which could not sleep for the chattering of birds, set up a beast, whose head was like a dragon: and we which stand in awe of report, are compelled to set before our owl Pallas shield, thinking by her virtue to cover the other's deformity. It was a sign of famine to Egypt, when Nilus flowed less than twelve cubits, or more than eighteen: and it may threaten despair unto us, if we be less courteous than you look for, or more cumbersome. But as Theseus being promised to be brought to an eagle's nest, and travailing all the day, found but a wren in a hedge, yet said, "this is a bird": so we hope, if the shower of our swelling mountain seem to bring forth some elephant, perform but a mouse, you will gently say, "this is a beast". Basil softly touched, yieldeth a sweet scent, but chafed in the hand, a rank savour: we fear even so that our labours slyly glanced on, will breed some content, but examined to the proof, small commendation. The haste in performing shall be our excuse. There went two nights to the begetting of Hercules. Feathers appear not on the phoenix under seven months, and the mulberry is twelve in budding: but our travails are like the hare's, who at one time bringeth forth, nourisheth, and engendreth again; or like the brood of trochilus, whose eggs in the same moment that they are laid, become birds. But howsoever we finish our work, we crave pardon, if we offend in matter, and patience if we transgress in manners. We have mixed mirth with counsel, and discipline with delight, thinking it not amiss in the same garden to sow pot-herbs, that we set flowers. But we hope, as harts that cast their horns, snakes their skins, eagles their bills, become more fresh for any other labour: so our charge being shaken off, we shall be fit for greater matters. But lest like the Myndans, we make our gates greater than our town, and that our play runs out at the preface, we here conclude: wishing that although there be in your precise judgments an universal mislike, yet we may enjoy by your wonted courtesies a general silence.

THE PROLOGUE AT THE COURT

We are ashamed that our bird, which fluttered by twilight seeming a swan, should be proved a bat set against the sun. But as Jupiter placed Silenus' ass among the stars, and Alcebiades covered his pictures being owls and apes, with a curtain embroidered with lions and eagles, so are we enforced upon a rough discourse to draw on a smooth excuse; resembling lapidaries, who think to hide the crack in a stone by setting it deep in gold. The gods supped once with poor Baucis, the Persian kings sometimes shaved sticks: our hope is your Highness will at this time lend an ear to an idle pastime. Appion raising Homer from hell, demanded only who was his father, and we calling Alexander from his grave, seek only who was his love.

Whatsoever we present, we wish it may be thought the dancing of Agrippa his shadows, who in the moment they were seen, were of any shape one would conceive: or lynxes, who having a quick sight to discern, have a short memory to forget. With us it is like to fare, as with these torches, which giving light to others, consume themselves: and we shewing delight to others, shame ourselves.

ACT I

SCENE I

Outside the walls of Athens.

Enter **CLYTUS** and **PARMENIO**.

CLYTUS
Parmenio, I cannot tell whether I should more commend in Alexander's victories, courage, or courtesy, in the one being a resolution without fear, in the other a liberality above custom: Thebes is razed, the people not racked, towers thrown down, bodies not thrust aside, a conquest without conflict, and a cruel war in a mild peace.

PARMENIO
Clytus, it becommeth the son of Philip to be none other than Alexander is: therefore seeing in the father a full perfection, who could have doubted in the son an excellency? For as the moon can borrow nothing else of the sun but light, so of a sire, in whom nothing but virtue was, what could the child receive but singular? It is for turqies to stain each other, not for diamonds; in the one to be made a difference in goodness, in the other no comparison.

CLYTUS
You mistake me Parmenio, if whilest I commend Alexander, you imagine I call Philip into question; unless happily you conjecture (which none of judgment will conceive) that because I like the fruit, therefore I heave at the tree; or coveting to kiss the child, I therefore go about to poison the teat.

PARMENIO
Ay, but Clytus, I perceive you are borne in the east, and never laugh but at the sun rising; which argueth though a duty where you ought, yet no great devotion where you might.

CLYTUS
We will make no controversy of that which there ought to be no question; only this shall be the opinion of us both, that none was worthy to be the father of Alexander but Philip, nor any meet to be the son of Philip but Alexander.

PARMENIO
Soft, Clytus, behold the spoils and prisoners! A pleasant sight to us, because profit is joined with honour; not much painful to them, because their captivity is eased by mercy.

[Enter **TIMOCLEA**, **CAMPASPE**, with other **CAPTIVES**, and spoils, **GUARDED**.

TIMOCLEA
Fortune, thou didst never yet deceive virtue, because virtue never yet did trust fortune. Sword and fire will never get spoil, where wisdom and fortitude bears sway. O Thebes, thy walls were raised by the sweetness of the harp, but razed by the shrillness of the trumpet. Alexander had never come so near the walls, had Epaminondas walked about the walls: and yet might the Thebans have been merry in their streets, if he had been to watch their towers. But destiny is seldom foreseen, never prevented. We are here now captives, whose necks are yoked by force, but whose hearts cannot yield by death. Come Campaspe and the rest, let us not be ashamed to cast our eyes on him, on whom we feared not to cast our darts.

PARMENIO
Madame, you need not doubt, it is Alexander, that is the conqueror.

TIMOCLEA
Alexander hath overcome, not conquered.

PARMENIO
To bring all under his subjection is to conquer.

TIMOCLEA
He cannot subdue that which is divine.

PARMENIO
Thebes was not.

TIMOCLEA
Virtue is.

CLYTUS
Alexander as he tendreth virtue, so he will you; he drinketh not blood, but thirsteth after honour; he is greedy of victory, but never satisfied with mercy. In fight terrible, as becommeth a captain; in conquest mild, as beseemeth a king. In all things then which nothing can be greater, he is Alexander.

CAMPASPE

Then if it be such a thing to be Alexander, I hope it shall be no miserable thing to be a virgin. For if he save our honours, it is more than to restore our goods. And rather do I wish he preserve our fame than our lives; which if he do, we will confess there can be no greater thing than to be Alexander.

[Enter **ALEXANDER**, **HEPHESTION**, and **ATTENDANTS**.

ALEXANDER
Clytus, are these prisoners? of whence these spoils?

CLYTUS
Like your Majesty, they are prisoners, and of Thebes.

ALEXANDER
Of what calling or reputation?

CLYTUS
I know not, but they seem to be ladies of honour.

ALEXANDER
I will know: madam, of whence you are I know; but who, I cannot tell.

TIMOCLEA
Alexander, I am the sister of Theagines, who fought a battle with thy father before the city of Chyronie, where he died, I say which none can gainsay, valiantly.

ALEXANDER
Lady, there seem in your words sparks of your brother's deeds, but worser fortune in your life than his death: but fear not, for you shall live without violence, enemies, or necessity: but what are you fair lady, another sister to Theagines?

CAMPASPE
No sister to Theagines, but an humble hand-maid to Alexander, born of a mean parentage, but to extreme fortune.

ALEXANDER
Well ladies, for so your virtues shew you, whatsoever your births be, you shall be honourably entreated. Athens shall be your Thebes, and you shall not be as abjects of war, but as subjects to Alexander. Parmenio, conduct these honourable ladies into the city: charge the soldiers not so much as in words to offer them any offence, and let all wants be supplied, so far forth as shall be necessary for such persons and my prisoners.

[Exeunt **PARMENIO** et **CAPTIVI**.

Hephestion, it resteth now that we have as great care to govern in peace, as conquer in war: that whilest arms cease, arts may flourish, and joining letters with lances, we endeavour to be as good philosophers as soldiers, knowing it no less praise to be wise, than commendable to be valiant.

HEPHESTION

Your Majesty therein sheweth that you have as great desire to rule as to subdue: and needs must that commonwealth be fortunate, whose captain is a philosopher, and whose philosopher is a captain.

[Exeunt.

SCENE II

A street.

Enter **MANES, GRANICHUS, PSYLLUS.**

MANES
I serve instead of a master, a mouse, whose house is a tub, whose dinner is a crust, and whose bed is a board.

PSYLLUS
Then art thou in a state of life which philosophers commend. A crumb for thy supper, an hand for thy cup, and thy clothes for thy sheets. For natura paucis contenta.

GRANICHUS
Manes, it is pity so proper a man should be cast away upon a philosopher: but that Diogenes that dog should have Manes that dogbolt, it grieveth nature and spiteth art: the one having found thee so dissolute, absolute I would say, in body, the other so single, singular in mind.

MANES
Are you merry? it is a sign by the trip of your tongue, and the toys of your head, that you have done that today, which I have not done these three days.

PSYLLUS
What is that?

MANES
Dined.

GRANICHUS
I think Diogenes keeps but cold cheer.

MANES
I would it were so, but he keepeth neither hot nor cold.

GRANICHUS
What then, lukewarm? That made Manes run from his master the last day.

PSYLLUS
Manes had reason: for his name foretold as much.

MANES
My name? how so, sir boy?

PSYLLUS
You know that it is called Mons, à movendo, because it stands still.

MANES
Good.

PSYLLUS
And thou art named Manes, à manendo, because thou runnest away.

MANES
Passing reasons! I did not run away, but retire.

PSYLLUS
To a prison, because thou wouldst have leisure to contemplate.

MANES
I will prove that my body was immortal: because it was in prison.

GRANICHUS
As how?

MANES
Did your masters never teach you that the soul is immortal?

GRANICHUS
Yes.

MANES
And the body is the prison of the soul.

GRANICHUS
True.

MANES
Why then, thus to make my body immortal, I put it to prison.

GRANICHUS
Oh bad!

PSYLLUS
Excellent ill!

MANES

You may see how dull a fasting wit is: therefore, Psyllus, let us go to supper with Granichus: Plato is the best fellow of all philosophers. Give me him that reads in the morning in the school, and at noon in the kitchen.

PSYLLUS
And me.

GRANICHUS
Ah sirs, my master is a king in his parlour for the body, and a god in his study for the soul. Among all his men he commendeth one that is an excellent musician, then stand I by, and clap another on the shoulder, and say, "this is a passing good cook."

MANES
It is well done Granichus; for give me pleasure that goes in at the mouth, not the ear; I had rather fill my guts than my brains.

PSYLLUS
I serve Apelles, who feedeth me as Diogenes doth Manes; for at dinner the one preacheth abstinence, the other commendeth counterfeiting: when I would eat meat, he paints a spit, and when I thirst, saith he, "is not this a fair pot?" and points to a table which contains the banquet of the gods, where are many dishes to feed the eye, but not to fill the gut.

GRANICHUS
What doest thou then?

PSYLLUS
This doeth he then, bring in many examples that some have lived by savours, and proveth that much easier it is to fat by colours: and tells of birds that have been fatted by painted grapes in winter: and how many have so fed their eyes with their mistress' picture, that they never desired to take food, being glutted with the delight in their favours. Then doth he shew me counterfeits, such as have surfeited with their filthy and loathsome vomits, and with the riotous bacchanalles of the god Bacchus, and his disorderly crew, which are painted all to the life in his shop. To conclude, I fare hardly, though I go richly, which maketh me when I should begin to shadow a lady's face, to draw a lamb's head, and sometimes to set to the body of a maid a shoulder of mutton: for semper animus meus est in patinis.

MANES
Thou art a god to me: for could I see but a cook's shop painted, I would make mine eyes fat as butter. For I have nought but sentences to fill my maw, as plures occidit crapula quàm gladius: musa ieiunantibus amica: "repletion killeth delicately": and an old saw of abstinence by Socrates: "the belly is the head's grave". Thus with sayings, not with meat, he maketh a gallimaufry.

GRANICHUS
But how doest thou then live?

MANES
With fine jests, sweet air, and the dog's alms.

GRANICHUS

Well, for this time I will stanch thy gut, and among pots and platters thou shalt see what it is to serve Plato.

PSYLLUS
For joy of it Granichus let's sing.

MANES
My voice is as clear in the evening as in the morning.

GRANICHUS
Another commodity of emptiness.

SONG.

GRANICHUS
O for a bowl of fat canary,
Rich Palermo, sparkling sherry,
Some nectar else, from Juno's dairy,
O these draughts would make us merry.

PSYLLUS
O for a wench, (I deal in faces,
And in other daintier things,)
Tickled am I with her embraces,
Fine dancing in such fairy rings.

MANES
O for a plump fat leg of mutton,
Veal, lamb, capon, pig, and cony,
None is happy but a glutton,
None an ass, but who wants money.

CHORUS
Wines (indeed,) and girls are good,
But brave victuals feast the blood,
For wenches, wine, and lusty cheer,
Jove would leap down to surfeit here.

[Exeunt.

SCENE III

Interior of the Palace.

[Enter **MELIPPUS**.

MELIPPUS

I had never such ado to warn scholars to come before a king. First, I came to Chrysippus, a tall lean old mad man, willing him presently to appear before Alexander; he stood staring on my face, neither moving his eyes nor his body; I urging him to give some answer, he took up a book, sat down and said nothing: Melissa his maid told me it was his manner, and that oftentimes she was fain to thrust meat into his mouth: for that he would rather starve than cease study. Well, thought I, seeing bookish men are so blockish, and great clerks such simple courtiers, I will neither be partaker of their commons nor their commendations. From thence I came to Plato and to Aristotle, and to diverse other, none refusing to come, saving an old obscure fellow, who sitting in a tub turned towards the sun, read Greek to a young boy; him when I willed to appear before Alexander, he answered, if Alexander would fain see me, let him come to me; if learn of me, let him come to me; whatsoever it be, let him come to me: why, said I, he is a king; he answered, why I am a philosopher; why, but he is Alexander; ay, but I am Diogenes. I was half angry to see one so crooked in his shape, to be so crabbed in his sayings. So going my way, I said, thou shalt repent it, if thou comest not to Alexander: nay, smiling answered he, Alexander may repent it, if he come not to Diogenes: virtue must be sought, not offered: and so turning himself to his cell, he grunted I know not what, like a pig under a tub. But I must be gone, the philosophers are coming.

[Exit.

[Enter **PLATO**, **ARISTOTLE**, **CLEANTHES**, **ANAXARCHUS**, **CRATES**, and **CHRYSIPPUS**.

PLATO

It is a difficult controversy, Aristotle, and rather to be wondered at than believed, how natural causes should work supernatural effects.

ARISTOTLE

I do not so much stand upon the apparition is seen in the moon, neither the demonium of Socrates, as that I cannot by natural reason give any reason of the ebbing and flowing of the sea, which makes me in the depth of my studies to cry out, O ens entium, miserere mei.

PLATO

Cleanthes and you attribute so much to nature by searching for things which are not to be found, that whilest you study a cause of your own, you omit the occasion itself. There is no man so savage in whom resteth not this divine particle, that there is an omnipotent, eternal, and divine mover, which may be called God.

CLEANTHES

I am of this mind, that that first mover, which you term God, is the instrument of all the movings which we attribute to nature. The earth which is mass, swimmeth on the sea, seasons divided in themselves, fruits growing in themselves, the majesty of the sky, the whole firmament of the world, and whatsoever else appeareth miraculous, what man almost of mean capacity but can prove it natural?

ANAXARCHUS

These causes shall be debated at our philosophers' feast, in which controversy I will take part with Aristotle, that there is Natura naturans, and yet not God.

CRATES

And I with Plato, that there is Deus optimus maximus, and not nature.

ARISTOTLE
Here commeth Alexander.

[Enter **ALEXANDER**, **HEPHESTION**, **PARMENIO** and **CLYTUS**.

ALEXANDER
I see, Hephestion, that these philosophers are here attending for us.

HEPHESTION
They are not philosophers, if they know not their duties.

ALEXANDER
But I much marvel Diogenes should be so dogged.

HEPHESTION
I do not think but his excuse will be better than Melippus' message.

ALEXANDER
I will go see him Hephestion, because I long to see him that would command Alexander to come, to whom all the world is like to come. Aristotle and the rest, sithence my coming from Thebes to Athens, from a place of conquest to a palace of quiet, I have resolved with myself in my court to have as many philosophers, as I had in my camp soldiers. My court shall be a school wherein I will have used as great doctrine in peace, as I did in war discipline.

ARISTOTLE
We are all here ready to be commanded, and glad we are that we are commanded: for that nothing better becometh kings than literature, which maketh them come as near to the gods in wisdom, as they do in dignity.

ALEXANDER
It is so Aristotle, but yet there is among you, yea and of your bringing up, that sought to destroy Alexander: Calistenes, Aristotle, whose treasons against his prince shall not be borne out with the reasons of his philosophy.

ARISTOTLE
If ever mischief entered into the heart of Calistenes, let Calistenes suffer for it; but that Aristotle ever imagined any such thing of Calistenes, Aristotle doth deny.

ALEXANDER
Well Aristotle, kindred may blind thee, and affection me; but in kings' causes I will not stand to scholars' arguments. This meeting shall be for a commandment, that you all frequent my court, instruct the young with rules, confirm the old with reasons: let your lives be answerable to your learnings, lest my proceedings be contrary to my promises.

HEPHESTION
You said you would ask every one of them a question, which yester-night none of us could answer.

ALEXANDER
I will. Plato, of all beasts, which is the subtlest?

PLATO
That which man hitherto never knew.

ALEXANDER
Aristotle, how should a man be thought a god?

ARISTOTLE
In doing a thing unpossible for a man.

ALEXANDER
Chrysippus, which was first, the day or the night?

CHRYSIPPUS
The day, by a day.

ALEXANDER
Indeed! strange questions must have strange answers. Cleanthes, what say you, is life or death the stronger?

CLEANTHES
Life, that suffereth so many troubles.

ALEXANDER
Crates, how long should a man live?

CRATES
Till he think it better to die than to live.

ALEXANDER
Anaxarchus, whether doth the sea or the earth bring forth most creatures?

ANAXARCHUS
The earth, for the sea is but a part of the earth.

ALEXANDER
Hephestion, me thinks they have answered all well, and in such questions I mean often to try them.

HEPHESTION
It is better to have in your court a wise man, than in your ground a golden mine. Therefore would I leave war, to study wisdom, were I Alexander.

ALEXANDER
So would I, were I Hephestion. But come, let us go and give release, as I promised to our Theban thralls.

[Exeunt **ALEXANDER, HEPHESTION, PARMENIO** and **CLYTUS**.

PLATO
Thou art fortunate Aristotle, that Alexander is thy scholar.

ARISTOTLE
And all you happy that he is your sovereign.

CHRYSIPPUS
I could like the man well, if he could be contented to be but a man.

ARISTOTLE
He seeketh to draw near to the gods in knowledge, not to be a god.

[Diogenes' tub is thrust on.

PLATO
Let us question a little with Diogenes, why he went not with us to Alexander. Diogenes, thou didst forget thy duty, that thou wentst not with us to the king.

DIOGENES [From his tub]
And you your profession, that you went to the king.

PLATO
Thou takest as great pride to be peevish, as others do glory to be virtuous.

DIOGENES
And thou as great honour being a philosopher to be thought court-like, as others shame that be courtiers, to be accounted philosophers.

ARISTOTLE
These austere manners set aside, it is well known that thou didst counterfeit money.

DIOGENES
And thou thy manners, in that thou didst not counterfeit money.

ARISTOTLE
Thou hast reason to contemn the court, being both in body and mind too crooked for a courtier.

DIOGENES
As good be crooked, and endeavor to make myself straight from the court, as be straight, and learn to be crooked at the court.

CRATES
Thou thinkest it a grace to be opposite against Alexander.

DIOGENES
And thou to be jump with Alexander.

ANAXARCHUS
Let us go: for in contemning him, we shall better please him, than in wondering at him.

ARISTOTLE
Plato, what dost thou think of Diogenes?

PLATO
To be Socrates, furious. Let us go.

[Exeunt **PHILOSOPHERS**.

ACT II

SCENE I

A street.

Enter on one side **DIOGENES**, with a lantern; on the other **PSYLLUS**, **MANES**, **GRANICHUS**.

PSYLLUS
Behold, Manes, where thy master is; seeking either for bones for his dinner, or pins for his sleeves. I will go salute him.

MANES
Do so; but mum, not a word that you saw Manes.

GRANICHUS
Then stay thou behind, and I will go with Psyllus.

PSYLLUS
All hail Diogenes to your proper person.

DIOGENES
All hate to thy peevish conditions.

GRANICHUS
O dog!

PSYLLUS
What doest thou seek for here?

DIOGENES
For a man and a beast.

GRANICHUS

That is easy without thy light to be found, be not all these men?

DIOGENES
Called men.

GRANICHUS
What beast is it thou lookest for?

DIOGENES
The beast my man, Manes.

PSYLLUS
He is a beast indeed that will serve thee.

DIOGENES
So is he that begat thee.

GRANICHUS
What wouldest thou do, if thou shouldest find Manes?

DIOGENES
Give him leave to do as he hath done before.

GRANICHUS
What's that?

DIOGENES
To run away.

PSYLLUS
Why, hast thou no need of Manes?

DIOGENES
It were a shame for Diogenes to have need of Manes, and for Manes to have no need of Diogenes.

GRANICHUS
But put the case he were gone, wouldst thou entertain any of us two?

DIOGENES
Upon condition.

PSYLLUS
What?

DIOGENES
That you should tell me wherefore any of you both were good.

GRANICHUS

Why, I am a scholar, and well seen in philosophy.

PSYLLUS
And I a prentice, and well seen in painting.

DIOGENES
Well then Granichus, be thou a painter to amend thine ill face; and thou Psyllus a philosopher to correct thine evil manners. But who is that, Manes?

MANES
I care not who I were, so I were not Manes.

GRANICHUS
You are taken tardy.

PSYLLUS
Let us slip aside Granichus, to see the salutation between Manes and his master.

DIOGENES
Manes, thou knowest the last day I threw away my dish, to drink in my hand, because it was superfluous; now I am determined to put away my man, and serve myself: Quia non egeo tui vel te.

MANES
Master, you know a while ago I ran away, so do I mean to do again, quia scio tibi non esse argentum.

DIOGENES
I know I have no money, neither will have ever a man: for I was resolved long sithence to put away both my slaves, money and Manes.

MANES
So was I determined to shake off both my dogs, hunger and Diogenes.

PSYLLUS
O sweet consent between a crowd and a Jew's harp.

GRANICHUS
Come, let us reconcile them.

PSYLLUS
It shall not need: for this is their use, now do they dine one upon another.

[Exit **DIOGENES**.

GRANICHUS
How now Manes, art thou gone from thy master?

MANES
No, I did but now bind myself to him.

PSYLLUS
Why you were at mortal jars.

MANES
In faith no, we brake a bitter jest one upon another.

GRANICHUS
Why thou art as dogged as he.

PSYLLUS
My father knew them both little whelps.

MANES
Well, I will hie me after my master.

GRANICHUS
Why, is it supper time with Diogenes?

MANES
Ay, with him at all time when he hath meat.

PSYLLUS
Why then, every man to his home, and let us steal out again anon.

GRANICHUS
Where shall we meet?

PSYLLUS
Why, at Alæ vendibili suspense hedera non est opus.

MANES
O Psyllus, habeo te loco parentis, thou blessest me.

[Exeunt.

SCENE II

Interior of the Palace.

Enter **ALEXANDER**, **HEPHESTION**, and **PAGE**.

ALEXANDER
Stand aside sir boy, till you be called. Hephestion, how do you like the sweet face of Campaspe?

HEPHESTION

I cannot but commend the stout courage of Timoclea.

ALEXANDER
Without doubt Campaspe had some great man to her father.

HEPHESTION
You know Timoclea had Theagines to her brother.

ALEXANDER
Timoclea still in thy mouth! art thou not in love?

HEPHESTION
Not I.

ALEXANDER
Not with Timoclea you mean; wherein you resemble the lapwing, who cryeth most where her nest is not. And so you lead me from espying your love with Campaspe, you cry Timoclea.

HEPHESTION
Could I as well subdue kingdoms, as I can my thoughts; or were I as far from ambition, as I am from love; all the world would account me as valiant in arms, as I know myself moderate in affection.

ALEXANDER
Is love a vice?

HEPHESTION
It is no virtue.

ALEXANDER
Well, now shalt thou see what small difference I make between Alexander and Hephestion. And sith thou hast been always partaker of my triumphs, thou shalt be partaker of my torments. I love, Hephestion, I love! I love Campaspe, a thing far unfit for a Macedonian, for a king, for Alexander. Why hangest thou down thy head Hephestion? blushing to hear that which I am not ashamed to tell.

HEPHESTION
Might my words crave pardon, and my counsel credit, I would both discharge the duty of a subject, for so I am, and the office of a friend, for so I will.

ALEXANDER
Speak Hephestion; for whatsoever is spoken, Hephestion speaketh to Alexander.

HEPHESTION
I cannot tell, Alexander, whether the report be more shameful to be heard, or the cause sorrowful to be believed? What! is the son of Philip, king of Macedon, become the subject of Campaspe, the captive of Thebes? Is that mind, whose greatness the world could not contain, drawn within the compass of an idle alluring eye? Will you handle the spindle with Hercules, when you should shake the spear with Achilles? Is the warlike sound of drum and trump turned to the soft noise of lyre and lute? the neighing of barbed steeds, whose loudness filled the air with terror, and whose breaths dimmed the sun with smoke,

converted to delicate tunes and amorous glances? O Alexander, that soft and yielding mind should not be in him, whose hard and unconquered heart hath made so many yield. But you love,—ah grief! but whom? Campaspe? Ah shame! a maid forsooth unknown, unnoble, and who can tell whether immodest? whose eyes are framed by art to enamour, and whose heart was made by nature to enchant. Ay, but she is beautiful; yea, but not therefore chaste: ay, but she is comely in all parts of the body: but she may be crooked in some part of the mind: ay, but she is wise, yea, but she is a woman! Beauty is like the blackberry, which seemeth red, when it is not ripe, resembling precious stones that are polished with honey, which the smoother they look, the sooner they break. It is thought wonderful among the seamen, that mugill, of all fishes the swiftest, is found in the belly of the bret, of all the slowest: And shall it not seem monstrous to wisemen, that the heart of the greatest conquerour of the world, should be found in the hands of the weakest creature of nature? of a woman? of a captive? Hermyns have fair skins, but foul livers; sepulchers fresh colours, but rotten bones; women fair faces, but false hearts. Remember, Alexander, thou hast a camp to govern, not a chamber; fall not from the armour of Mars to the arms of Venus; from the fiery assaults of war, to the maidenly skirmishes of love; from displaying the eagle in thine ensign, to set down the sparrow. I sigh, Alexander, that where fortune could not conquer, folly should overcome. But behold all the perfection that may be in Campaspe; a hair curling by nature, not art; sweet alluring eyes; a fair face made in despite of Venus, and a stately port in disdain of Juno; a wit apt to conceive, and quick to answer; a skin as soft as silk, and as smooth as jet; a long white hand, a fine little foot; to conclude, all parts answerable to the best part – what of this? Though she have heavenly gifts, virtue and beauty, is she not of earthly metal, flesh and blood? You, Alexander, that would be a god, shew yourself in this worse than a man, so soon to be both overseen and overtaken in a woman, whose false tears know their true times, whose smooth words wound deeper than sharp swords. There is no surfeit so dangerous as that of honey, nor any poison so deadly as that of love; in the one physic cannot prevail, nor in the other counsel.

ALEXANDER
My case were light, Hephestion, and not worthy to be called love, if reason were a remedy, or sentences could salve, that sense cannot conceive. Little do you know, and therefore slightly do you regard, the dead embers in a private person, or live coals in a great prince, whose passions and thoughts do as far exceed others in extremity, as their callings do in majesty. An eclipse in the sun is more than the falling of a star; none can conceive the torments of a king, unless he be a king, whose desires are not inferior to their dignities. And then judge, Hephestion, if the agonies of love be dangerous in a subject, whether they be not more than deadly unto Alexander, whose deep and not to be conceived sighs, cleave the heart in shivers; whose wounded thoughts can neither be expressed nor endured. Cease then, Hephestion, with arguments to seek to refel that, which with their deity the gods cannot resist; and let this suffice to answer thee, that it is a king that loveth, and Alexander, whose affections are not to be measured by reason, being immortal, nor I fear me to be borne, being intolerable.

HEPHESTION
I must needs yield, when neither reason nor counsel can be heard.

ALEXANDER
Yield, Hephestion, for Alexander doth love, and therefore must obtain.

HEPHESTION
Suppose she loves not you; affection commeth not by appointment or birth; and then as good hated as enforced.

ALEXANDER
I am a king, and will command.

HEPHESTION
You may, to yield to lust by force; but to consent to love by fear, you cannot.

ALEXANDER
Why, what is that which Alexander may not conquer as he list?

HEPHESTION
Why, that which you say the gods cannot resist, love.

ALEXANDER
I am a conquerour, she a captive; I as fortunate, as she fair: my greatness may answer her wants, and the gifts of my mind, the modesty of hers: is it not likely then that she should love? Is it not reasonable?

HEPHESTION
You say that in love there is no reason, and therefore there can be no likelihood.

ALEXANDER
No more, Hephestion: in this case I will use mine own counsel, and in all other thine advice; thou mayst be a good soldier, but never good lover. Call my page.

[**PAGE** advances.

Sirrah, go presently to Apelles, and will him to come to me without either delay or excuse.

PAGE
I go.

[The tub is thrust on.

ALEXANDER
In the mean season to recreate my spirits, being so near, we will go see Diogenes. And see where his tub is. Diogenes!

DIOGENES
Who calleth?

ALEXANDER
Alexander: how happened it that you would not come out of your tub to my palace?

DIOGENES
Because it was as far from my tub to your palace, as from your palace to my tub.

ALEXANDER
Why then doest thou owe no reverence to kings?

DIOGENES

No.

ALEXANDER

Why so?

DIOGENES

Because they be no gods.

ALEXANDER

They be gods of the earth.

DIOGENES

Yea, gods of earth.

ALEXANDER

Plato is not of thy mind.

DIOGENES

I am glad of it.

ALEXANDER

Why?

DIOGENES

Because I would have none of Diogenes' mind, but Diogenes.

ALEXANDER

If Alexander have any thing that may pleasure Diogenes, let me know, and take it.

DIOGENES

Then take not from me that you cannot give me, the light of the world.

ALEXANDER

What doest thou want?

DIOGENES

Nothing that you have.

ALEXANDER

I have the world at command.

DIOGENES

And I in contempt.

ALEXANDER

Thou shalt live no longer than I will.

DIOGENES
But I shall die whether you will or no.

ALEXANDER
How should one learn to be content?

DIOGENES
Unlearn to covet.

ALEXANDER
Hephestion, were I not Alexander, I would wish to be Diogenes.

HEPHESTION
He is dogged, but discreet; I cannot tell how sharp, with a kind of sweetness; full of wit, yet too too wayward.

ALEXANDER
Diogenes, when I come this way again, I will both see thee, and confer with thee.

DIOGENES
Do.

[Re-enter **PAGE** with **APELLES**.

ALEXANDER
But here commeth Apelles: how now Apelles, is Venus' face yet finished?

APELLES
Not yet: beauty is not so soon shadowed, whose perfection commeth not within the compass either of cunning or of colour.

ALEXANDER
Well, let it rest unperfect, and come you with me, where I will shew you that finished by nature, that you have been trifling about by art.

[Exeunt.

ACT III

SCENE I

A room in Apelles' house.

[Enter **APELLES**, **CAMPASPE** and **PSYLLUS**.

APELLES

Lady, I doubt whether there be any colour so fresh, that may shadow a countenance so fair.

CAMPASPE
Sir, I had thought you had been commanded to paint with your hand, not to gloss with your tongue; but as I have heard, it is the hardest thing in painting to set down a hard favour, which maketh you to despair of my face; and then shall you have as great thanks to spare your labour, as to discredit your art.

APELLES
Mistress, you neither differ from yourself nor your sex: for knowing your own perfection, you seem to dispraise that which men most commend, drawing them by that mean into an admiration, where feeding themselves they fall into an ecstasy; your modesty being the cause of the one, and of the other, your affections.

CAMPASPE
I am too young to understand your speech, though old enough to withstand your device: you have been so long used to colours, you can do nothing but colour.

APELLES
Indeed the colours I see, I fear will alter the colour I have: but come madam, will you draw near, for Alexander will be here anon. Psyllus, stay you here at the window, if any enquire for me, answer, Non lubet esse domi.

[Exeunt into studio.

SCENE II

The same.

Enter **PSYLLUS**.

PSYLLUS
It is always my master's fashion, when any fair gentlewoman is to be drawn within, to make me to stay without. But if he should paint Jupiter like a bull, like a swan, like an eagle, then must Psyllus with one hand grind colours, and with the other hold the candle. But let him alone, the better he shadows her face, the more will he burn his own heart. And now if any man could meet with Manes, who, I dare say, looks as lean as if Diogenes dropped out of his nose—

[Enter **MANES**.

MANES
And here comes Manes, who hath as much meat in his maw, as thou hast honesty in thy head.

PSYLLUS
Then I hope thou art very hungry.

MANES

They that know thee, know that.

PSYLLUS
But dost thou not remember that we have certain licour to confer withal.

MANES
Ay, but I have business; I must go cry a thing.

PSYLLUS
Why, what hast thou lost?

MANES
That which I never had, my dinner.

PSYLLUS
Foul lubber, wilt thou cry for thy dinner?

MANES
I mean, I must cry; not as one would say cry, but cry, that is make a noise.

PSYLLUS
Why fool, that is all one; for if thou cry, thou must needs make a noise.

MANES
Boy, thou art deceived. Cry hath diverse significations, and may be alluded to many things; knave but one, and can be applied but to thee.

PSYLLUS
Profound Manes!

MANES
We Cynics are mad fellows, didst thou not find I did quip thee?

PSYLLUS
No verily! why, what's a quip?

MANES
We great girders call it a short saying of a sharp wit, with a bitter sense in a sweet word.

PSYLLUS
How canst thou thus divine, divide, define, dispute, and all on the sudden?

MANES
Wit will have his swing; I am bewitched, inspired, inflamed, infected.

PSYLLUS
Well, then will not I tempt thy gibing spirit.

MANES

Do not Psyllus, for thy dull head will be but a grindstone for my quick wit, which if thou whet with overthwarts, perjisti, actum est de te. I have drawn blood at one's brains with a bitter bob.

PSYLLUS

Let me cross myself: for I die, if I cross thee.

MANES

Let me do my business, I myself am afraid, lest my wit should wax warm, and then must it needs consume some hard head with fine and pretty jests. I am sometimes in such a vain, that for want of some dull pate to work on, I begin to gird myself.

PSYLLUS

The gods shield me from such a fine fellow, whose words melt wits like wax.

MANES

Well then, let us to the matter. In faith, my master meaneth tomorrow to fly.

PSYLLUS

It is a jest.

MANES

Is it a jest to fly? shouldest thou fly so, soon thou shouldest repent it in earnest.

PSYLLUS

Well, I will be the cryer.

MANES and **PSYLLUS** [One after another]

O ys! O ys!

O ys! All manner of men, women, or children, that will come tomorrow into the market place, between the hours of nine and ten, shall see Diogenes the Cynic fly.

PSYLLUS

I do not think he will fly.

MANES

Tush, say fly.

PSYLLUS

Fly.

MANES

Now let us go: for I will not see him again till midnight, I have a back way into his tub.

PSYLLUS

Which way callest thou the back way, when every way is open?

MANES

I mean to come in at his back.

PSYLLUS
Well, let us go away, that we may return speedily.

[Exeunt.

SCENE III

The same.

The curtains of the central structure are withdrawn, discovering the studio within.

Enter **APELLES, CAMPASPE**.

APELLES
I shall never draw your eyes well, because they blind mine.

CAMPASPE
Why then, paint me without eyes, for I am blind.

APELLES
Were you ever shadowed before of any?

CAMPASPE
No. And would you could so now shadow me, that I might not be perceived of any.

APELLES
It were pity, but that so absolute a face should furnish Venus' temple amongst these pictures.

CAMPASPE
What are these pictures?

APELLES
This is Leda, whom Jove deceived in likeness of a swan.

CAMPASPE
A fair woman, but a foul deceit.

APELLES
This is Alcmena, unto whom Jupiter came in shape of Amphitrion her husband, and begat Hercules.

CAMPASPE
A famous son, but an infamous fact.

APELLES

He might do it, because he was a god.

CAMPASPE
Nay, therefore it was evil done, because he was a god.

APELLES
This is Danae, into whose prison Jupiter drizzled a golden shower, and obtained his desire.

CAMPASPE
What gold can make one yield to desire?

APELLES
This is Europa, whom Jupiter ravished; this Antiopa.

CAMPASPE
Were all the gods like this Jupiter?

APELLES
There were many gods in this like Jupiter.

CAMPASPE
I think in those days love was well ratified among men on earth, when lust was so full authorized by the gods in Heaven.

APELLES
Nay, you may imagine there were women passing amiable, when there were Gods exceeding amorous.

CAMPASPE
Were women never so fair, men would be false.

APELLES
Were women never so false, men would be fond.

CAMPASPE
What counterfeit is this, Apelles?

APELLES
This is Venus, the goddess of love.

CAMPASPE
What, be there also loving goddesses?

APELLES
This is she that hath power to command the very affections of the heart.

CAMPASPE
How is she hired: by prayer, by sacrifice, or bribes?

APELLES
By prayer, sacrifice, and bribes.

CAMPASPE
What prayer?

APELLES
Vows irrevocable.

CAMPASPE
What sacrifice?

APELLES
Hearts ever sighing, never dissembling.

CAMPASPE
What bribes?

APELLES
Roses and kisses: but were you never in love?

CAMPASPE
No, nor love in me.

APELLES
Then have you injuried many!

CAMPASPE
How so?

APELLES
Because you have been loved of many.

CAMPASPE
Flattered perchance of some.

APELLES
It is not possible that a face so fair, and a wit so sharp, both without comparison, should not be apt to love.

CAMPASPE
If you begin to tip your tongue with cunning, I pray dip your pencil in colours; and fall to that you must do, not that you would do.

[The curtains close.

SCENE IV

The Palace.

Enter **CLYTUS** and **PARMENIO**.

CLYTUS
Parmenio, I cannot tell how it commeth to pass, that in Alexander nowadays there groweth an unpatient kind of life: in the morning he is melancholy, at noon solemn; at all times either more sour or severe, than he was accustomed.

PARMENIO In kings' causes I rather love to doubt than conjecture, and think it better to be ignorant than inquisitive: they have long ears and stretched arms, in whose heads suspicion is a proof, and to be accused is to be condemned.

CLYTUS
Yet between us there can be no danger to find out the cause: for that there is no malice to withstand it. It may be an unquenchable thirst of conquering maketh him unquiet: it is not unlikely his long ease hath altered his humour: that he should be in love, it is not impossible.

PARMENIO
In love, Clytus? no, no, it is as far from his thought, as treason in ours: he, whose ever waking eye, whose never tired heart, whose body patient of labour, whose mind unsatiable of victory hath always been noted, cannot so soon be melted into the weak conceits of love. Aristotle told him there were many worlds, and that he hath not conquered one that gapeth for all, galleth Alexander. But here he commeth.

[Enter **ALEXANDER** and **HEPHESTION**.

ALEXANDER
Parmenio and Clytus, I would have you both ready to go into Persia about an embassage no less profitable to me, than to yourselves honourable.

CLYTUS
We are ready at all commands; wishing nothing else, but continually to be commanded.

ALEXANDER
Well, then withdraw yourselves, till I have further
considered of this matter.

[Exeunt **CLYTUS** and **PARMENIO**.

Now we will see how Apelles goeth forward: I doubt me that nature hath overcome art, and her countenance his cunning.

HEPHESTION
You love, and therefore think anything.

ALEXANDER

But not so far in love with Campaspe as with Bucephalus, if occasion serve either of conflict or of conquest.

HEPHESTION

Occasion cannot want, if will do not. Behold all Persia swelling in the pride of their own power; the Scythians careless what courage or fortune can do; the Egyptians dreaming in the soothsayings of their augurs, and gaping over the smoke of their beasts' entrails. All these, Alexander, are to be subdued, if that world be not slipped out of your head, which you have sworn to conquer with that hand.

[During the following speech the tub is thrust on, from which appears Diogenes, to whom enters **CYRSUS**.

ALEXANDER

I confess the labour's fit for Alexander, and yet recreation necessary among so many assaults, bloody wounds, intolerable troubles: give me leave a little, if not to sit, yet to breath. And doubt not but Alexander can, when he will, throw affections as far from him as he can cowardice. But behold Diogenes talking with one at his tub.

CYRSUS

One penny, Diogenes, I am a Cynic.

DIOGENES

He made thee a begger, that first gave thee anything.

CYRSUS

Why, if thou wilt give nothing, nobody will give thee.

DIOGENES

I want nothing, till the springs dry, and the earth perish.

CYRSUS

I gather for the gods.

DIOGENES

And I care not for those gods which want money.

CYRSUS

Thou art not a right Cynic that will give nothing.

DIOGENES

Thou art not, that will beg anything.

CYRSUS

Alexander, King Alexander, give a poor Cynic a groat.

ALEXANDER

It is not for a king to give a groat.

CYRSUS
Then give me a talent.

ALEXANDER
It is not for a begger to ask a talent. Away! Apelles?

[The curtains open, discovering the studio with **APELLES** and **CAMPASPE**.

APELLES
Here.

ALEXANDER
Now, gentlewoman, doth not your beauty put the painter to his trump?

CAMPASPE
Yes my lord, seeing so disordered a countenance, he feareth he shall shadow a deformed counterfeit.

ALEXANDER
Would he could colour the life with the feature. And me thinketh, Apelles, were you as cunning as report saith you are, you may paint flowers as well with sweet smells as fresh colours, observing in your mixture such things as should draw near to their savours.

APELLES
Your majesty must know, it is no less hard to paint savours, than virtues; colours can neither speak nor think.

ALEXANDER
Where do you first begin, when you draw any picture?

APELLES
The proposition of the face in just compass, as I can.

ALEXANDER
I would begin with the eye, as a light to all the rest.

APELLES
If you will paint, as you are a king, your majesty may begin where you please; but as you would be a painter, you must begin with the face.

ALEXANDER
Aurelius would in one hour colour four faces.

APELLES
I marvel in half an hour he did not four.

ALEXANDER
Why, is it so easy?

APELLES

No, but he doth it so homely.

ALEXANDER

When will you finish Campaspe?

APELLES

Never finish: for always in absolute beauty there is somewhat above art.

ALEXANDER

Why should not I by labour be as cunning as Apelles?

APELLES

God shield you should have cause to be so cunning as Apelles!

ALEXANDER

Me thinketh four colours are sufficient to shadow any countenance, and so it was in the time of Phydias.

APELLES

Then had men fewer fancies, and women not so many favours. For now, if the hair of her eye-brows be black, yet must the hair of her head be yellow: the attire of her head must be different from the habit of her body, else would the picture seem like the blazon of ancient armory, not like the sweet delight of new found amiableness. For as in garden knots diversity of odours make a more sweet savour, or as in music divers strings cause a more delicate consent, so in painting, the more colours, the better counterfeit, observing black for a ground, and the rest for grace.

ALEXANDER

Lend me thy pencil Apelles, I will paint, and thou shalt judge.

APELLES

Here.

ALEXANDER

The coal breaks.

APELLES

You lean too hard.

ALEXANDER

Now it blacks not.

APELLES

You lean too soft.

ALEXANDER

This is awry.

APELLES
Your eye goeth not with your hand.

ALEXANDER
Now it is worse.

APELLES
Your hand goeth not with your mind.

ALEXANDER
Nay, if all be too hard or soft, so many rules and regards, that one's hand, one's eye, one's mind must all draw together, I had rather be setting of a battle than blotting of a board. But how have I done here?

APELLES
Like a king.

ALEXANDER
I think so: but nothing more unlike a painter. Well Apelles, Campaspe is finished as I wish, dismiss her, and bring presently her counterfeit after me.

APELLES
I will.

[**ALEXANDER** and **HEPHESTION** come from the studio.

ALEXANDER
Now Hephestion, doth not this matter cotton as I would? Campaspe looketh pleasantly, liberty will increase her beauty, and my love shall advance her honour.

HEPHESTION
I will not contrary your majesty, for time must wear out that love hath wrought, and reason wean what appetite nursed.

[**CAMPASPE** comes from the studio.

ALEXANDER
How stately she passeth by, yet how soberly! A sweet consent in her countenance with a chaste disdain, desire mingled with coyness, and I cannot tell how to term it, a curst yielding modesty!

HEPHESTION
Let her pass.

ALEXANDER
So she shall for the fairest on the earth.

[Exeunt.

SCENE V

The same.

Enter **PSYLLUS** and **MANES**.

PSYLLUS
I shall be hanged for tarrying so long.

MANES
I pray God my master be not flown before I come.

PSYLLUS
Away Manes! my master doth come.

[Exit **MANES**. **APELLES** comes from the studio.

APELLES
Where have you been all this while?

PSYLLUS
Nowhere but here.

APELLES
Who was here since my coming?

PSYLLUS
Nobody.

APELLES
Ungracious wag, I perceive you have been a-loitering; was Alexander nobody?

PSYLLUS
He was a king, I meant no mean body.

APELLES
I will cudgel your body for it, and then will I say it was nobody, because it was no honest body. Away in!

[Exit **PSYLLUS**.

Unfortunate Apelles, and therefore unfortunate because Apelles! Hast thou by drawing her beauty brought to pass that thou canst scarce draw thine own breath? And by so much the more hast thou increased thy care, by how much the more thou hast shewed thy cunning: was it not sufficient to behold the fire and warm thee, but with Satyrus thou must kiss the fire and burn thee? O Campaspe, Campaspe, art must yield to nature, reason to appetite, wisdom to affection. Could Pigmalion entreat by prayer to have his ivory turned into flesh? and cannot Apelles obtain by plaints to have the picture of his love changed to life? Is painting so far inferior to carving? or dost thou Venus more delight to be hewed with chisels, than shadowed with colours? What Pigmalion, or what Pyrgoteles, or what Lysippus is he, that ever made thy face so fair, or spread thy fame so far as I? unless Venus, in this thou enviest mine art, that in colouring my sweet Campaspe, I have left no place by cunning to make thee so amiable. But alas! she is the paramour to a prince. Alexander the monarch of the earth hath both her body and affection. For what is it that kings cannot obtain by prayers, threats and promises? Will not she think it better to sit under a cloth of estate like a queen, than in a poor shop like a huswife? and esteem it sweeter to be the concubine of the lord of the world, than spouse to a painter in Athens? Yes, yes, Apelles, thou mayest swim against the stream with the crab, and feed against the wind with the deer, and peck against the steel with the cockatrice: stars are to be looked at, not reached at: princes to be yielded unto, not contended with: Campaspe to be honoured, not obtained, to be painted, not possessed of thee. O fair face! O unhappy hand! and why didst thou draw it so fair a face? O beautiful countenance, the express image of Venus, but somewhat fresher: the only pattern of that eternity, which Jupiter dreaming of asleep, could not conceive again waking. Blush Venus, for I am ashamed to end thee. Now must I paint things unpossible for mine art, but agreeable with my affections: deep and hollow sighs, sad and melancholy thoughts, wounds and slaughters of conceits, a life posting to death, a death galloping from life, a wavering constancy, an unsettled resolution, and what not, Apelles? And what but Apelles? But as they that are shaken with a fever are to be warmed with clothes, not groans, and as he that melteth in a consumption is to be recured by colices, not conceits: so the feeding canker of my care, the never dying worm of my heart, is to be killed by counsel, not cries, by applying of remedies, not by replying of reasons. And sith in cases desperate there must be used medicines that are extreme, I will hazard that little life that is left, to restore the greater part that is lost, and this shall be my first practise: for wit must work, where authority is not. As soon as Alexander hath viewed this portraiture, I will by devise give it a blemish, that by that means she may come again to my shop; and then as good it were to utter my love, and die with denial, as conceal it, and live in despair.

[Song by **APELLES**.
Cupid and my Campaspe played
At cards for kisses, Cupid paid;
He stakes his quiver, bow, and arrows,
His mother's doves, and team of sparrows;
Loses them too; then, down he throws
The corral of his lip, the rose
Growing on's cheek (but none knows how),
With these, the crystal of his brow,
And then the dimple of his chin:
All these did my Campaspe win.
At last, he set her both his eyes;
She won, and Cupid blind did rise.
O love! has she done this to thee?
What shall (Alas!) become of me?

[Exit.

ACT IV

SCENE I

The Market-place, with Diogenes' tub.

Enter **SOLINUS**, **PSYLLUS**, and **GRANCHUS**.

SOLINUS
This is the place, the day, the time, that Diogenes hath appointed to fly.

PSYLLUS
I will not lose the flight of so fair a foul as Diogenes is, though my master cudgel my no-body, as he threatened.

GRANICHUS
What Psyllus, will the beast wag his wings today?

PSYLLUS
We shall hear: for here commeth Manes: Manes will it be?

[Enter **MANES**.

MANES
Be! he were best be as cunning as a bee, or else shortly he will not be at all.

GRANICHUS
How is he furnished to fly, hath he feathers?

MANES
Thou art an ass! capons, geese, and owls have feathers. He hath found Dedalus' old waxen wings, and hath been piecing them this month, he is so broad in the shoulders. O you shall see him cut the air even like a tortoise.

SOLINUS
Me thinks so wise a man should not be so mad, his body must needs be too heavy.

MANES
Why, he hath eaten nothing this sevennight but cork and feathers.

PSYLLUS [Aside]
Touch him, Manes.

MANES
He is so light, that he can scarce keep him from flying at midnight. Populus intrat.

MANES
See, they begin to flock, and behold my master bustles himself to fly.

[**DIOGENES** comes out of his tub.

DIOGENES

You wicked and bewitched Athenians, whose bodies make the earth to groan, and whose breaths infect the air with stench. Come ye to see Diogenes flie? Diogenes commeth to see you sink: ye call me dog: so I am, for I long to gnaw the bones in your skins. Ye term me a hater of men: no, I am a hater of your manners. Your lives dissolute, not fearing death, will prove your deaths desperate, not hoping for life: what do you else in Athens but sleep in the day, and surfeit in the night: back gods in the morning with pride, in the evening belly gods with gluttony! You flatter kings, and call them gods, speak truth of yourselves, and confess you are devils! From the bee you have taken not the honey, but the wax, to make your religion, framing it to the time, not to the truth. Your filthy lust you colour under a courtly colour of love, injuries abroad under the title of policies at home, and secret malice creepeth under the name of public justice. You have caused Alexander to dry up springs and plant vines, to sow rocket and weed endiff, to shear sheep, and shrine foxes. All conscience is seeled at Athens. Swearing commeth of a hot mettle: lying of a quick wit: flattery of a flowing tongue: undecent talk of a merry disposition. All things are lawful at Athens. Either you think there are no gods, or I must think ye are no men. You build as though you should live forever, and surfeit as though you should die tomorrow. None teacheth true philosophy but Aristotle, because he was the king's schoolmaster! O times! O men! O corruption in manners! Remember that green grass must turn to dry hay. When you sleep, you are not sure to wake; and when you rise, not certain to lie down. Look you never so high, your heads must lie level with your feet. Thus have I flown over your disordered lives, and if you will not amend your manners, I will study to fly further from you, that I may be nearer to honesty.

SOLINUS

Thou ravest, Diogenes, for thy life is different from thy words. Did not I see thee come out of a brothel house? was it not a shame?

DIOGENES

It was no shame to go out, but a shame to go in.

GRANICHUS

It were a good deed, Manes, to beat thy master.

MANES

You were as good eat my master. One of the people. Hast thou made us all fools, and wilt thou not fly?

DIOGENES

I tell thee, unless thou be honest, I will fly.

PEOPLE

Dog! dog! take a bone!

DIOGENES

Thy father need fear no dogs, but dogs thy father.

PEOPLE

We will tell Alexander, that thou reprovest him behind his back.

DIOGENES

And I will tell him, that you flatter him before his face.

PEOPLE

We will cause all the boys in the street to hiss at thee.

DIOGENES

Indeed I think the Athenians have their children ready for any vice, because they be Athenians.

MANES

Why master, mean you not to fly?

DIOGENES

No, Manes, not without wings.

MANES

Everybody will account you a liar.

DIOGENES

No, I warrant you; for I will always say the Athenians are mischievous.

PSYLLUS

I care not, it was sport enough for me to see these old huddles hit home.

GRANICHUS

Nor I.

PSYLLUS

Come, let us go! and hereafter when I mean to rail upon any body openly, it shall be given out, I will fly.

[Exeunt.

SCENE II

A room in Apelles' house, as before.

Enter **CAMPASPE**.

CAMPASPE [sola]

Campaspe, it is hard to judge whether thy choice be more unwise, or thy chance unfortunate. Dost thou prefer – but stay, utter not that in words, which maketh thine ears to glow with thoughts. Tush! better thy tongue wag, than thy heart break! Hath a painter crept further into thy mind than a prince? Apelles, than Alexander? Fond wench! the baseness of thy mind bewrays the meanness of thy birth. But alas! affection is a fire, which kindleth as well in the bramble as in the oak; and catcheth hold where it first lighteth, not where it may best burn. Larks that mount aloft in the air, build their nests below in the earth; and women that cast their eyes upon kings, may place their hearts upon vassals. A needle will become thy fingers better than a lute, and a distaff is fitter for thy hand than a scepter. Ants live safely, till they have gotten wings, and juniper is not blown up till it hath gotten an high top. The mean estate is without care as long as it continueth without pride. But here commeth Apelles, in whom I would there were the like affection.

[Enter **APELLES**.

APELLES
Gentlewoman, the misfortune I had with your picture, will put you to some pains to sit again to be painted.

CAMPASPE
It is small pains for me to sit still, but infinite for you to draw still.

APELLES
No madam! to paint Venus was a pleasure, but to shadow the sweet face of Campaspe it is a heaven!

CAMPASPE
If your tongue were made of the same flesh that your heart is, your words would be as your thoughts are: but such a common thing it is amongst you to commend, that oftentimes for fashion sake you call them beautiful, whom you know black.

APELLES
What might men do to be believed?

CAMPASPE
Whet their tongue on their hearts.

APELLES
So they do, and speak as they think.

CAMPASPE
I would they did!

APELLES
I would they did not!

CAMPASPE
Why, would you have them dissemble?

APELLES
Not in love, but their love. But will you give me leave to ask you a question without offence?

CAMPASPE
So that you will answer me another without excuse.

APELLES
Whom do you love best in the world?

CAMPASPE

He that made me last in the world.

APELLES
That was a god.

CAMPASPE
I had thought it had been a man: But whom do you honour most, Apelles?

APELLES
The thing that is likest you, Campaspe.

CAMPASPE
My picture?

APELLES
I dare not venture upon your person. But come, let us go in: for Alexander will think it long till we return.

[Exeunt.

SCENE III

A room in the Palace

Enter **CLYTUS** and **PARMENIO**.

CLYTUS
We hear nothing of our embassage, a colour belike to blear our eyes, or tickle our ears, or inflame our hearts. But what doth Alexander in the mean season, but use for tantara, sol, fa, la, for his hard couch, down beds, for his handful of water, his standing cup of wine?

PARMENIO
Clytus, I mislike this new delicacy and pleasing peace: for what else do we see now than a kind of softness in every mans mind; bees to make their hives in soldiers' helmets; our steeds furnished with footcloths of gold, instead of saddles of steel: more time to be required to scour the rust of our weapons, than there was wont to be in subduing the countries of our enemies. Sithence Alexander fell from his hard armour to his soft robes, behold the face of his court: youths that were wont to carry devises of victory in their shields, engrave now posies of love in their rings: they that were accustomed on trotting horses to charge the enemy with a lance, now in easy coaches ride up and down to court ladies; instead of sword and target to hazard their lives, use pen and paper to paint their loves. Yea, such a fear and faintness is grown in court, that they wish rather to hear the blowing of a horn to hunt, than the sound of a trumpet to fight. O Philip, wert thou alive to see this alteration, thy men turned to women, thy soldiers to lovers, gloves worn in velvet caps, instead of plumes in graven helmets, thou wouldest either die among them for sorrow, or confound them for anger.

CLYTUS

Cease, Parmenio, lest in speaking what becommeth thee not, thou feel what liketh thee not: truth is never without a scratched face, whose tongue although it cannot be cut out, yet must it be tied up.

PARMENIO
It grieveth me not a little for Hephestion, who thirsteth for honour, not ease; but such is his fortune and nearness in friendship to Alexander, that he must lay a pillow under his head, when he would put a target in his hand. But let us draw in, to see how well it becomes them to tread the measures in a dance, that were wont to set the order for a march.

[Exeunt.

SCENE IV

Apelles' studio.

APELLES and **CAMPASPE** are discovered.

APELLES
I have now, Campaspe, almost made an end.

CAMPASPE
You told me, Apelles, you would never end.

APELLES
Never end my love: for it shall be eternal.

CAMPASPE
That is, neither to have beginning nor ending.

APELLES
You are disposed to mistake, I hope you do not mistrust.

CAMPASPE
What will you say if Alexander perceive your love?

APELLES
I will say it is no treason to love.

CAMPASPE
But how if he will not suffer thee to see my person?

APELLES
Then will I gaze continually on thy picture.

CAMPASPE
That will not feed thy heart.

APELLES

Yet shall it fill mine eye: besides the sweet thoughts, the sure hopes, thy protested faith, will cause me to embrace thy shadow continually in mine arms, of the which by strong imagination I will make a substance.

CAMPASPE

Well, I must be gone: but this assure yourself, that I had rather be in thy shop grinding colours, than in Alexander's court, following higher fortunes.

[Exit **APELLES**.

CAMPASPE [alone]

Foolish wench, what hast thou done? that, alas! which cannot be undone, and therefore I fear me undone. But content is such a life, I care not for abundance. O Apelles, thy love commeth from the heart, but Alexander's from the mouth. The love of kings is like the blowing of winds, which whistle sometimes gently among the leaves, and straight ways turn the trees up by the roots; or fire which warmeth afar off, and burneth near hand; or the sea, which maketh men hoise their sails in a flattering calm, and to cut their masts in a rough storm. They place affection by times, by policy, by appointment; if they frown, who dares call them unconstant? if bewray secrets, who will term them untrue? if fall to other loves, who trembles not, if he call them unfaithful? In kings there can be no love, but to queens: for as near must they meet in majesty, as they do in affection. It is requisite to stand aloof from kings' love, Jove, and lightning.

[Exit.

SCENE V

The same.

Enter **APELLES** from the studio.

APELLES

Now Apelles, gather thy wits together: Campaspe is no less wise then fair, thyself must be no less cunning then faithful. It is no small matter to be rival with Alexander.

[Enter **PAGE**.

PAGE

Apelles, you must come away quickly with the picture; the king thinketh that now you have painted it, you play with it.

APELLES

If I would play with pictures, I have enough at home.

PAGE

None perhaps you like so well.

APELLES
It may be I have painted none so well.

PAGE
I have known many fairer faces.

APELLES
And I many better boys.

[Exeunt.

ACT V

SCENE I

The Market-place, with Diogenes' tub.

Enter **SYLVIUS, PERIM, MILO, TRICO,** and **MANES** to **DIOGENES.**

SYLVIUS
I have brought my sons, Diogenes, to be taught of thee.

DIOGENES
What can thy sons do?

SYLVIUS
You shall see their qualities: Dance, sirrah!

[Then **PERIM** danceth.

How like you this: doth he well?

DIOGENES
The better, the worser.

SYLVIUS
The music very good.

DIOGENES
The musicians very bad; who only study to have their strings in tune, never framing their manners to order.

SYLVIUS
Now shall you see the other. Tumble, sirrah!

[**MILO** tumbleth.

How like you this? why do you laugh?

DIOGENES
To see a wag that was born to break his neck by destiny, to practise it by art.

MILO
This dog will bite me, I will not be with him.

DIOGENES
Fear not, boy, dogs eat no thistles.

PERIM
I marvel what dog thou art, if thou be a dog.

DIOGENES
When I am hungry, a mastiff; and when my belly is full, a spaniel.

SYLVIUS
Dost thou believe that there are any gods, that thou art so dogged?

DIOGENES
I must needs believe there are gods: for I think thee an enemy to them.

SYLVIUS
Why so?

DIOGENES
Because thou hast taught one of thy sons to rule his legs, and not to follow learning; the other to bend his body every way, and his mind no way.

PERIM
Thou doest nothing but snarl, and bark like a dog.

DIOGENES
It is the next way to drive away a thief.

SYLVIUS
Now shall you hear the third, who sings like a nightingale.

DIOGENES
I care not: for I have a nightingale to sing herself.

SYLVIUS
Sing, sirrah!

[**TRICO** singeth.

Song.

What bird so sings, yet so does wail?
O t'is the ravished nightingale.
Jug, jug, jug, jug, tereu, she cries,
And still her woes at midnight rise.
Brave prick song! who is't now we hear?
None but the lark so shrill and clear;
How at Heaven's gates she claps her wings,
The morn not waking till she sings.
Hark, hark, with what a pretty throat
Poor robin red-breast tunes his note;
Hark how the jolly cuckoos sing
Cuckoo, to welcome in the spring;
Cuckoo, to welcome in the spring.

SYLVIUS
Lo, Diogenes! I am sure thou canst not do so much.

DIOGENES
But there is never a thrush but can.

SYLVIUS
What hast thou taught Manes thy man?

DIOGENES
To be as unlike as may be thy sons.

MANES
He hath taught me to fast, lie hard, and run away.

SYLVIUS
How sayest thou Perim, wilt thou be with him?

PERIM
Ay, so he will teach me first to run away.

DIOGENES
Thou needest not be taught, thy legs are so nimble.

SYLVIUS
How sayest thou Milo, wilt thou be with him?

DIOGENES
Nay, hold your peace, he shall not.

SYLVIUS
Why?

DIOGENES
There is not room enough for him and me to tumble both in one tub.

SYLVIUS
Well, Diogenes, I perceive my sons brook not thy manners.

DIOGENES
I thought no less, when they knew my virtues.

SYLVIUS
Farewell Diogenes, thou neededst not have scraped roots, if thou wouldest have followed Alexander.

DIOGENES
Nor thou have followed Alexander, if thou hadst scraped roots.

[Exeunt.

SCENE II

The same.

Enter **APELLES**.

APELLES [Alone]
I fear me, Apelles, that thine eyes have blabbed that, which thy tongue durst not. What little regard hadst thou! whilst Alexander viewed the counterfeit of Campaspe, thou stoodest gazing on her countenance. If he espy or but suspect, thou must needs twice perish, with his hate, and thine own love. Thy pale looks when he blushed, thy sad countenance when he smiled, thy sighs when he questioned, may breed in him a jealousy, perchance a frenzy. O love! I never before knew what thou wert, and now hast thou made me that I know not what myself am? only this I know, that I must endure intolerable passions, for unknown pleasures. Dispute not the cause, wretch, but yield to it: for better it is to melt with desire, than wrestle with love. Cast thyself on thy careful bed, be content to live unknown, and die unfound. O Campaspe, I have painted thee in my heart: painted? nay, contrary to mine art, imprinted; and that in such deep characters, that nothing can rase it out, unless it rub my heart out.

[Exit.

SCENE III

The same.

Enter **MILECTUS, PHRYGIUS, LAIS,** to **DIOGENES** in his tub.

MILECTUS
It shall go hard, but this peace shall bring us some pleasure.

PHRYGIUS
Down with arms, and up with legs, this is a world for the nonce.

LAIS
Sweet youths, if you knew what it were to save your sweet blood, you would not so foolishly go about to spend it. What delight can there be in gashing, to make foul scars in fair faces, and crooked maims in straight legs? as though men being born goodly by nature, would of purpose become deformed by folly; and all forsooth for a new found term, called valiant, a word which breedeth more quarrels than the sense can commendation.

MILECTUS
It is true, Lais, a featherbed hath no fellow, good drink makes good blood, and shall pelting words spill it?

PHRYGIUS
I mean to enjoy the world, and to draw out my life at the wiredrawer's, not to curtall it off at the cutler's.

LAIS
You may talk of war, speak big, conquer worlds with great words: but stay at home, where instead of alarums you shall have dances, for hot battles with fierce men, gentle skirmishes with fair women. These pewter coats can never sit so well as satin doublets. Believe me, you cannot conceive the pleasure of peace, unless you despise the rudeness of war.

MILECTUS
It is so. But see Diogenes prying over his tub:
Diogenes, what sayest thou to such a morsel?

DIOGENES
I say, I would spit it out of my mouth, because it should not poison my stomach.

PHRYGIUS
Thou speakest as thou art, it is no meat for dogs.

DIOGENES
I am a dog, and philosophy rates me from carrion.

LAIS
Uncivil wretch, whose manners are answerable to thy calling, the time was thou wouldest have had my company, had it not been, as thou saidst, too dear.

DIOGENES
I remember there was a thing that I repented me of, and now thou hast told it; indeed it was too dear of nothing, and thou dear to nobody.

LAIS
Down, villain! or I will have thy head broken.

MILECTUS
Will you couch?

PHRYGIUS
Avant, cur! Come, sweet Lais, let us go to some place, and possess peace. But first let us sing, there is more pleasure in tuning of a voice, than in a volley of shot.

[Song.

MILECTUS
Now let us make haste, lest Alexander find us here.

[Exeunt.

SCENE IV

The same.

Enter **ALEXANDER**, **HEPHESTION**, and **PAGE**.

ALEXANDER
Me thinketh, Hephestion, you are more melancholy than you were accustomed; but I perceive it is all for Alexander. You can neither brook this peace, nor my pleasure; be of good cheer, though I wink, I sleep not.

HEPHESTION
Melancholy I am not, nor well content: for I know not how, there is such a rust crept into my bones with this long ease, that I fear I shall not scour it out with infinite labours.

ALEXANDER
Yes, yes, if all the travails of conquering the world will set either thy body or mine in tune, we will undertake them. But what think you of Apelles? Did ye ever see any so perplexed? He neither answered directly to any question, nor looked steadfastly upon anything. I hold my life the painter is in love.

HEPHESTION
It may be: for commonly we see it incident in artificers to be enamoured of their own works, as Archidamus of his wooden dove, Pygmalion of his ivory image, Arachne of his wooden swan; especially painters, who playing with their own conceits, now coveting to draw a glancing eye, then a-rolling, now a-winking, still mending it, never ending it, till they be caught with it; and then poor souls they kiss the colours with their lips, with which before they were loth to taint their fingers.

ALEXANDER

I will find it out. Page, go speedily for Apelles, will him to come hither, and when you see us earnestly in talk, suddenly cry out, "Apelles' shop is on fire!"

PAGE
It shall be done.

ALEXANDER
Forget not your lesson.

[Exit **PAGE**.

HEPHESTION
I marvel what your device shall be.

ALEXANDER
The event shall prove.

HEPHESTION
I pity the poor painter, if he be in love.

ALEXANDER
Pity him not, I pray thee; that severe gravity set aside, what do you think of love?

HEPHESTION
As the Macedonians do of their herb beet, which looking yellow in the ground, and black in the hand, think it better seen than touched.

ALEXANDER
But what do you imagine it to be?

HEPHESTION
A word by superstition thought a god, by use turned to an humour, by self-will made a flattering madness.

ALEXANDER
You are too hard hearted to think so of love. Let us go to Diogenes. Diogenes, thou may'st think it somewhat that Alexander commeth to thee again so soon.

DIOGENES
If you come to learn, you could not come soon enough; if to laugh, you be come too soon.

HEPHESTION
It would better become thee to be more courteous, and frame thyself to please.

DIOGENES
And you better to be less, if you durst displease.

ALEXANDER

What dost thou think of the time we have here?

DIOGENES
That we have little, and lose much.

ALEXANDER
If one be sick, what wouldst thou have him do?

DIOGENES
Be sure that he make not his physician his heir.

ALEXANDER
If thou mightest have thy will, how much ground would content thee?

DIOGENES
As much as you in the end must be contented withal.

ALEXANDER
What, a world?

DIOGENES
No, the length of my body.

ALEXANDER
Hephestion, shall I be a little pleasant with him?

HEPHESTION
You may: but he will be very perverse with you.

ALEXANDER
It skilleth not, I cannot be angry with him. Diogenes, I pray thee, what dost thou think of love?

DIOGENES
A little worser than I can of hate.

ALEXANDER
And why?

DIOGENES
Because it is better to hate the things which make to love, than to love the things which give occasion of hate.

ALEXANDER
Why, be not women the best creatures in the world?

DIOGENES
Next men and bees.

ALEXANDER
What dost thou dislike chiefly in a woman?

DIOGENES
One thing.

ALEXANDER
What?

DIOGENES
That she is a woman.

ALEXANDER
In mine opinion thou wert never born of a woman, that thou thinkest so hardly of women; but now commeth Apelles, who I am sure is as far from thy thoughts, as thou art from his cunning. Diogenes, I will have thy cabin removed nearer to my court, because I will be a philosopher.

DIOGENES
And when you have done so, I pray you remove your court further from my cabin, because I will not be a courtier.

[Enter **APELLES**.

ALEXANDER
But here commeth Apelles. Apelles, what piece of work have you now in hand?

APELLES
None in hand, if it like your majesty: but I am devising a platform in my head.

ALEXANDER
I think your hand put it in your head. Is it nothing about Venus?

APELLES
No, but something above Venus.

PAGE
Apelles, Apelles, look about you, your shop is on fire!

APELLES
Aye me! if the picture of Campaspe be burnt, I am undone!

ALEXANDER
Stay Apelles, no haste; it is your heart is on fire, not your shop; and if Campaspe hang there, I would she were burnt. But have you the picture of Campaspe? Belike you love her well, that you care not though all be lost, so she be safe.

APELLES

Not love her: but your majesty knows that painters in their last works are said to excel themselves, and in this I have so much pleased myself, that the shadow as much delighteth me being an artificer, as the substance doth others that are amorous.

ALEXANDER
You lay your colours grossly; though I could not paint in your shop, I can spy into your excuse. Be not ashamed Apelles, it is a gentleman's sport to be in love.
[To **ATTENDANTS**]
Call hither Campaspe. Methinks I might have been made privy to your affection; though my counsel had not been necessary, yet my countenance might have been thought requisite. But Apelles, forsooth, loveth under hand, yea and under Alexander's nose, and – but I say no more.

APELLES
Apelles loveth not so: but he liveth to do as Alexander will.

[Enter **CAMPASPE**.

ALEXANDER
Campaspe, here is news. Apelles is in love with you.

CAMPASPE
It pleaseth your majesty to say so.

ALEXANDER [Aside to **HEPHESTION**]
Hephestion, I will try her too. – Campaspe, for the good qualities I know in Apelles, and the virtue I see in you, I am determined you shall enjoy one another. How say you Campaspe, would you say "Ay"?

CAMPASPE
Your handmaid must obey, if you command.

ALEXANDER [Aside to **HEPHESTION**]
Think you not Hephestion, that she would fain be commanded?

HEPHESTION
I am no thought-catcher, but I guess unhappily.

ALEXANDER [To **CAMPASPE**]
I will not enforce marriage, where I cannot compel love.

CAMPASPE
But your majesty may move a question, where you be willing to have a match.

ALEXANDER
Believe me, Hephestion, these parties are agreed, they would have me both priest and witness. Apelles, take Campaspe; why move ye not? Campaspe, take Apelles; will it not be? If you be ashamed one of the other, by my consent you shall never come together. But dissemble not, Campaspe, do you love Apelles?

CAMPASPE
Pardon my lord, I love Apelles!

ALEXANDER
Apelles, it were a shame for you, being loved so openly of so fair a virgin, to say the contrary. Do you love Campaspe?

APELLES
Only Campaspe!

ALEXANDER
Two loving worms, Hephestion! I perceive Alexander cannot subdue the affections of men, thoughhe conquer their countries. Love falleth like a dew aswell upon the low grass, as upon the high cedar. Sparks have their heat, ants their gall, flies their spleen. Well, enjoy one another, I give her thee frankly, Apelles. Thou shalt see that Alexander maketh but a toy of love, and leadeth affection in fetters; using fancy as a fool to make him sport, or a minstrel to make him merry. It is not the amorous glance of an eye can settle an idle thought in the heart; no, no, it is children's game, a life for seamsters and scholars; the one pricking in clouts have nothing else to think on, the other picking fancies out of books, have little else to marvel at. Go, Apelles, take with you your Campaspe, Alexander is cloyed with looking on that which thou wond'rest at.

APELLES
Thanks to your majesty on bended knee, you have honoured Apelles.

CAMPASPE
Thanks with bowed heart, you have blessed Campaspe.

[Exit **APELLES** and **CAMPASPE**.

ALEXANDER
Page, go warn Clytus and Parmenio and the other lords to be in a readiness, let the trumpet sound, strike up the drum, and I will presently into Persia. How now, Hephestion, is Alexander able to resist love as he list?

HEPHESTION
The conquering of Thebes was not so honourable as the subduing of these thoughts.

ALEXANDER
It were a shame Alexander should desire to command the world, if he could not command himself. But come, let us go, I will try whether I can better bear my hand with my heart, than I could with mine eye. And good Hephestion, when all the world is won, and every country is thine and mine, either find me out another to subdue, or on my word I will fall in love.

[Exeunt.

THE EPILOGUE AT THE BLACKE FRYERS

Where the rainbow toucheth the tree, no caterpillars will hang on the leaves: where the glow-worm creepeth in the night, no adder will go in the day. We hope in the ears where our travails be lodged, no carping shall harbour in those tongues. Our exercises must be as your judgment is, resembling water, which is always of the same colour into what it runneth.

In the Trojan horse lay couched soldiers, with children; and in heaps of many words we fear diverse unfit, among some allowable. But as Demosthenes with often breathing up the hill amended his stammering; so we hope with sundry labours against the hair, to correct our studies. If the tree be blasted that blossoms, the fault is in the wind, and not in the root; and if our pastimes be misliked, that have been allowed, you must impute it to the malice of others, and not our endeavour. And so we rest in good case, if you rest well content.

THE EPILOGUE AT THE COURT

We cannot tell whether we are fallen among Diomedes' birds or his horses; the one received some men with sweet notes, the other bit all men with sharp teeth. But as Homer's gods conveyed them into clouds, whom they would have kept from curses, and as Venus, lest Adonis should be pricked with the stings of adders, covered his face with the wings of swans; so we hope, being shielded with your Highness' countenance, we shall, though we hear the neighing, yet not feel the kicking of those jades, and receive, though no praise (which we cannot deserve) yet a pardon, which in all humility we desire. As yet we cannot tell what we should term our labours, iron or bullion; only it belongeth to your Majesty to make them fit either for the forge, or the mint; current by the stamp, or counterfeit by the anvil. For as nothing is to be called white, unless it had been named white by the first creator, so can there be nothing thought good in the opinion of others, unless it be christened good by the judgment of yourself. For ourselves again, we are like these torches of wax, of which being in your Highness' hands, you may make doves or vultures, roses or nettles, laurel for a garland, or elder for a disgrace.

John Lyly – A Short Biography

John Lyly was born in Kent in 1553 or 1554, the eldest of eight children.

As can be imagined accurate records dating so far back for his early life are few and far between. It is most probable that Canterbury, Kent was his actual birthplace.

At age sixteen he became a student at Magdalen College, Oxford, and obtained his bachelor's degree in 1573 and his master's two years later. In 1574 he applied to Lord Burghley for the Queen's letters to admit him as a fellow at Magdalen College, but this was not granted, and Lyly subsequently left the university.

After Oxford, where he had the reputation of 'a noted wit', Lyly seems to have continued to advance his career through Lord Burghley. 'This noble man', he writes in the Glasse for Europe, in the second part of Euphues (1580), 'I found so ready being but a straunger to do me good, that neyther I ought to forget him, neyther cease to pray for him, that as he hath the wisdom of Nestor, so he may have the age, that having the policies of Ulysses he may have his honor, worthy to lyve long, by whom so many lyve in quiet, and not unworthy to be advaunced by whose care so many have been preferred.'

Lyly became the private secretary of Burghley's son-in-law, Edward de Vere, 17th Earl of Oxford, himself a playwright and to whom the second part of 'Euphues' is dedicated. De Vere seems to have acted as patron to most of Lyly's literary associates when they moved from Oxford to London to begin their careers in the commercial world.

He began his own literary career with 'Euphues', or 'The Anatomy of Wit', which was licensed to Gabriel Cawood in December 1578 and published the following spring. In the same year he was incorporated M.A. at the University of Cambridge. However, his hopes of an advancement at court were dashed with the appointment in July of Edmund Tylney to the office of Master of the Revels, a post on which he had set his sights.

'Euphues and his England' appeared in 1580, and, like the first part of the book, won immediate popularity. For a time Lyly was the most successful and fashionable of English writers, hailed as the author of 'a new English', as a 'raffineur de l'Anglois'; and, as Edward Blount, the editor of his plays, wrote in 1632, 'that beautie in court which could not parley Euphuism was as little regarded as she which nowe there speakes not French'.

After the publication of 'Euphues' Lyly changed literary direction; from writing novels to writing plays. Starting in 1580, Lyly received control over the Blackfriars Theatre, a commercial theatre which underlines both his commercial appeal and perhaps the reasoning for this change.

Two years later a letter from Lyly to the treasurer, in July 1582, protests the accusation of dishonesty which had brought him into trouble with his friend and patron, Edward de Vere, and demands a personal interview in order to clear his name. From accounts available despite his hopes and efforts Lyly failed to receive any significant patronage from either Burghley or Queen Elizabeth I.

His 'Campaspe' and 'Sapho and Phao' were produced at Court in 1582, perhaps through the Earl of Oxford's station as Lord High Chamberlain. In total, probably eight Lyly plays were acted before the queen by the Children of the Chapel and by the Children of Paul's between the years 1584 and 1591, and some were also repeated before a popular audience at the Blackfriars Theatre. Lyly used his talent for quick, lively dialogue, classical colour and frequent references to people and events of the day to sustain his popularity.

Lyle's importance as a playwright has brought with it conflicting views. His dialogue is by some distance removed from the mastery of Shakespeare but its advances in rapidity and resource are far better than anything which had gone before it; an important next step in the English dramatic art. His nimbleness, and the wit which struggles with his pedantry, found their full development with the Bard in the dialogue of 'Twelfth Night' and 'Much Ado about Nothing'. Indeed, it is Lyly's primary influence on the plays of Shakespeare which are to be applauded and in particular the romantic comedies. 'Love's Metamorphosis' has a clear influence on 'Love's Labour's Lost', as does 'Gallathea' on 'A Midsummer Night's Dream'.

In addition to the plays, Lyly also composed at least one 'entertainment' (a combination of elements from a masque and a drama) for Queen Elizabeth; 'The Entertainment at Chiswick' was staged on 28th and 29th July 1602. Lyly has been suggested as the author of several other royal entertainments of the 1590s, most probably 'The Entertainment at Mitcham' performed on 13th September 1598.

Aside from his writing Lyly also sat in parliament as a member for Hindon in Wiltshire in 1580, for Aylesbury in Buckinghamshire in 1593, for Appleby in Westmorland in 1597 and finally for Aylesbury again in 1601.

We know also that Lyly had married and the union produced two sons and a daughter. But when and to whom are not known.

In 1589 Lyly published anonymously a tract in the Martin Marprelate controversy, called 'Pappe with an hatchet, alias a figge for my Godsonne; Or Crack me this nut; Or a Countrie Cuffe, etc'.

About the same time he probably made his first of two petitions to Queen Elizabeth. The two petitions, transcripts of which are extant, are undated. In the first of them he speaks of ten years at court in the hope of preferment, and in the second he extends the period to thirteen years. It may be conjectured with great probability that the ten years date from 1579, when Tylney was appointed Master of the Revels with a tacit understanding that Lyly was to have the next reversion of the post. 'I was entertained your Majestie's servaunt by your own gratious favor', he says, 'strengthened with condicions that I should ayme all my courses at the Revells (I dare not say with a promise, but with a hopeful Item to the Revercion) for which these ten yeres I have attended with an unwearyed patience'. But the mastership of the revels was as far off as ever—Tylney would eventually hold the post for thirty-one years.

In the second petition of 1593, Lyly wrote 'Thirteen yeres your highnes servant but yet nothing. Twenty friends that though they saye they will be sure, I finde them sure to be slowe. A thousand hopes, but all nothing; a hundred promises but yet nothing. Thus casting up the inventory of my friends, hopes, promises and tymes, the summa totalis amounteth to just nothing'.

What may have been Lyly's subsequent fortunes at court are unknown. Blount says vaguely that Elizabeth 'graced and rewarded' him but brings to bear no other evidence.

After 1590 his works steadily declined in influence and reputation, although he continued to serve in parliament; in 1598 he served on a parliamentary committee about wine abuse.

In the early weeks of November 1606, John Lyly passed away from an unknown disease. He was buried in London at St Bartholomew-the-Less on 20th November 1606.

John Lyly – A Concise Bibliography

Writings

Euphues: The Anatomy of Wit (1578)
Euphues and His England (1580)
Pappe with an hatchet, alias a figge for my Godsonne; Or Crack me this nut; Or a Countrie Cuffe, etc. (1589)

Plays

In 1632 Blount published Six Court Comedies, the first printed collection of Lyly's plays. They appear in the following order with the date also of their separate publication in quarto form:

Endymion (1591)
Campaspe (1584)
Sapho and Phao (1584)
Gallathea (1592)
Midas (1592)
Mother Bombie (1594)

His other plays include:

Love's Metamorphosis (1601, possibly his earliest play, the surviving version a probable revision of the original)
The Woman in the Moon (1597)

These have been attributed to him but now thought doubtful:

A Warning for Faire Women (1599)
The Maid's Metamorphosis (1600)